PRAY FOR THE BEAR

FITFUNCARLY

MILFORD MA

PRAY FOR THE BEAR:
An Ordinary Person's Guide to
Unlocking Extraordinary Personal Strength
by Carly Fauth

© 2024 Carly Fauth
www.fitfuncarly.com

Published by FitFunCarly in
affiliation with Fearless Literary Services

ISBN: 979-8-218-51109-8

LIBRARY OF CONGRESS CONTROL NUMBER:
2024919805

COVER DESIGN
Carly Fauth & D. Patrick Miller

PRODUCTION & MANAGEMENT
D. Patrick Miller • Fearless Literary
www.fearlessbooks.com/Literary.html

TABLE OF CONTENTS

"If you see me in a fight with a bear, pray for the bear."

— KOBE BRYANT

Prologue

When I was eleven my Mormor (Danish for mother's mother) was dying of cancer. It was cancer of the duodenum. I remember our last Christmas Eve together, I had escaped the dining room table and snuck into the family room to hide under some blankets. Shortly after, my Mormor walked into the room and sat in a rocking chair by the crackling fire. She had no idea I was even there. I kept myself well hidden, but peeked out from under the blanket just to watch her rocking back and forth. As she stared into the flames, she had a very sad expression on her face. She kept closing her eyes as if she was completely exhausted, refusing to let herself fall asleep. She was wearing a brown wig that was meant to look like her own hair, but didn't quite meet that mark. The wig appeared to be slipping off; and that, for some reason, made me the most sad of all. I somehow knew this memory was important and would stay with me forever, so I just kept watching.

I remember wondering what she was feeling and desperately trying to put myself in her shoes. I knew she had cancer, but I didn't really understand what that word meant. All I knew was that she smoked, and that seemed to be the reason people got cancer. I'm not sure how long we were there, but I saw that when others came into the room, she adjusted her wig and sat up a little straighter. The tired woman I had seen staring into the flames was replaced by someone with a fierce determination to carry on.

At the end of the night I remember saying goodbye to my Mormor as she was pulling on her leather "driving gloves" she always wore to drive in the winter. Someone asked her if she was okay to drive, and I distinctly remember the look that flashed across her face as if she had been slapped. She didn't appreciate the fact that someone was simply taking away her freedom to do what she loved, so she snapped back, "Of course I can drive." In the awkward moment of silence that followed, the reality was that nobody in that room had ever experienced what she was going through. Although it felt impossible for us to understand, I remember really wanting to try.

My Mormor passed away later that year, and since then I have spent my life trying to hold on to her and feel the connection we once shared. I have been searching for her in other people, seeking signs from ladybugs, and trying to hear her whispering to me. Sadly, she has always felt so far away from me since then.

But not anymore. Now I see her, in my own eyes when I peer into the mirror. Thirty-seven years later, I feel the closeness I have been craving since she left me. Sitting where I am now, I completely understand what my

Mormor was feeling. I know the feeling of being so completely exhausted that rocking in a chair, staring at a flame, is the only thing you can imagine having the strength to do. I also know the feeling of well-intentioned people taking things away from you because they think they are making your life easier. I know that rage of wanting things to be different than they are and being envious of others who are thriving. I understand her pain. I understand her distance at times. I can relate to how she sometimes took her sadness out on other people.

I believe that my cancer diagnosis has been a way for me to make peace with the special relationship my Mormor and I lost out on 35 years ago. I feel a sense of relief from her, knowing that someone truly understands what she was going through and that anything she said or did during that time was just her way of coping.

I feel like I am finally bringing her some peace.

Mormor, this book is for you.

1

Find some good bricklayers.

This isn't my first book. When I was in second grade, I wrote my first book of short stories. It was called "The Fantasy Book". I wanted the title to be thrilling and something grownups would read. I remembered seeing the show "Fantasy Island" in the TV Guide and thinking I was definitely going to watch that when I grew up, so I borrowed the name for my book.

I vividly recall sitting at the lunch table for months with those small rectangular pieces of off-white paper feverishly writing down all the amazing stories in my head. I thought it was so cool that I could take something as abstract as a thought and put it down on paper so it was concrete and tangible. I collected all the sheets of paper in my Trapper Keeper and showed my mom one day.

My mom, always my biggest cheerleader, praised my stories and encouraged me to keep writing with the promise we could turn everything into a book. She told me to start illustrating and saved those drawings, too.

Once I had a collection, my mom kept her promise and brought me to the office of a family friend who had offered to make copies of "The Fantasy Book" and bind them. It was the most thrilling day of my eight years on the planet. I was actually an author! The experience is one I will never forget. I still have the book that made me an author, tucked away behind all of my socks in a drawer. When I reflect on this special memory, I recognize that the power of it is not just the fact that my mom did this wonderful thing for me, it's how she instilled something in me that created such a strong foundation of self-confidence by the way she did it.

My mom never corrected my spelling.

Truth be told, if you picked up the book, it would take you quite a while to understand what I was trying to say. However, my mom thought that was the beauty of it. She understood.

Instead of editing, my mom created an in-depth glossary at the back of the book to translate my way of sounding out the words. And when my chicken scratch illustrations barely made any sense, instead of asking me to add color or develop them a little more, she took my "I'm finished" with a nod of her head and said, "Looks good to me!"

She took my work and celebrated it for exactly what it was. She didn't push me to be "better" or tell me to practice more. She simply met me where I was at, cheered her heart out for me, and proudly shared my hard work with others. She called me an author and I believed her. It's because of this experience that I have continued my love of writing and felt confident enough to express my thoughts and feelings in words.

My mom has always been adding these types of bricks to my strong "sense of self" foundation. This foundation is what keeps me steady and strong when life's storms blow in. If you think back on your own life, I hope you can recognize the people who have been there adding bricks to your own foundation. If not, start now. Surround yourself with people who will celebrate and appreciate you for exactly who you are. No editing allowed.

2
Don't build walls.

There is a woman in my town who has political beliefs the exact opposite of mine. Over the years, I have found myself keeping a comfortable distance from her because I don't understand a lot of the things that she puts out there. Because of that, I have never really had the chance to get to know her on a personal level. My knowledge of her has basically come from her social media posts, which are on a completely different wavelength than mine. I think I have always been a little afraid of what may happen if she said something I didn't agree with. I don't really like confrontation, especially when it comes to discussing politics.

When I got sick, I received a lovely message from this woman, offering to make two of her family's favorite pasta dishes for my family. I had never really even had much of a conversation with her over the years, so I was a bit surprised. I thanked her and said we would love to be the recipient of her meals. She seemed just as happy that I said yes.

I will never forget the day she dropped off the dinner. Besides two large trays of homemade baked ziti and chicken with broccoli, bread and a salad, she also brought over disposable plates, napkins and cutlery so we didn't have any cleanup. Her son even baked brownies for us. In addition, she left a gift bag for me with epsom salts, Chapstick and word searches. I was so incredibly touched by her thoughtfulness and kindness. To be honest, it left me speechless. Out of all the people in the friend group we both were a part of, I thought she would be the last person to extend herself to us in that way. In fact, she turned out to be one of the only ones to offer.

If I am being completely honest, I would have never expected this incredible gesture from the type of person I had classified this woman to be in my head. The political landscape of this country favors division over unity, so it's easy to stereotype. I realized I was guilty of doing exactly what I get so frustrated about other people doing: I had built up a wall. I forgot that underneath it all, this woman was just as human as me and was made up of a lot more than just her political opinions.

Kindness and love can come from unexpected places. Make sure you are not building walls up in your mind to prevent that kind of light from shining in.

3

Be alone.

A fellow cancer warrior warned me that no matter how much love and support I am surrounded by during my journey, there will be times when I feel absolutely alone.

She was right.

However, it is during those times when it can feel a bit overwhelming, that I close my eyes and retreat to the sun-filled corners of my mind where my solitude is spent in a sanctuary of absolute bliss. I go to my bench in Denmark.

I walk down the hill and my bench comes into view, as if it's been patiently waiting for me since the last time I tearfully said, "See you again soon." I sit down, breathing in the summer scents of greenery and listening to the morning birds calling from the water. I stand up and run the dirt path that leads me through the winding woods. I continue along an empty airfield and head back to the water's edge. Finally, I reach the dock, where I slip off my sneakers, strip down to my bathing suit, and slowly descend down the steps of the ladder into the cold, crisp water. As I swim out, the peace and quiet take my breath away. All I can feel is the beating of my heart.

As I emerge from the water, I feel nothing but gratitude for this time and space.

When I open my eyes and my mind returns to my current reality, that warm and peaceful feeling remains steadfast.

We all need a special space and time to go to in the corner of our mind that belongs only to us. There are always going to be times when we feel alone and maybe a little bit scared. That's life. But, remembering those special times you created just for yourself will remind you that feeling alone is okay, and in fact, something to be grateful for.

Get out there today and be alone. Enjoy it. Fill a corner of your mind with a new place to retreat and embrace the feeling it brings.

4

Physically challenge yourself.

I don't mean to scare you.

But, if there is one thing I know for sure, it's that we all come up against something in our lifetime. Nobody escapes. Some of you reading this may be weathering a storm right now. Others of you may feel like you have been swimming against the current for years. Some days you may feel like you have it under control and other days you may feel like you're drowning.

There may be a couple of you, though, who have chosen to keep reading this because you may feel like life has been pretty easy for you, and you're wondering where I am going with this. It is to you that I am actually speaking. Enjoy this time. Don't feel guilty about it. But, at the same time, don't be shortsighted.

If you have not faced a situation in life that completely takes the wind out of your sails, it's imperative that you prepare for the challenge *now*. And fitness is the most practical and accessible way to start building the mental and physical strength you will need to not only get through, but **crush** whatever life throws at you.

I'm not saying you have to run to your computer and sign up for a 100-mile run or an Ironman. You can start exactly where you are. Maybe you challenge yourself to get off the couch and move TODAY. Or maybe you sign up for that dance class you have been wanting to try, but haven't felt confident enough to do yet. Or possibly you commit to doing 10 push-ups a day for a week to start building your upper body strength.

Every time we choose to physically challenge ourselves, we not only build strength in our body, we also strengthen our brain. We build confidence in our coping skills. We put ourselves in prime condition to fight the good fight. And WIN.

It's called grit.

5

You define you.

I made a decision. I chose to do something that many people don't quite know how to talk about or feel is appropriate to bring up. I did something that left me with a tight scar directly across my chest extending to underneath my armpits. It not only changed the way I look in my clothes, it eliminated an entire part of my wardrobe (peace out bras!).

The choice I made is one that many warned would leave me struggling with moments of grief. Others reassured me that I could "change my mind" and get "new ones" later. After all, all girls are supposed to have boobs, right?

"What does your husband think?" some have whispered, as if this is the most important question of all.

I came to a fork on a very scary road that no road map could help me navigate. I had to rely on my inner compass. Luckily for me, I have been fine tuning that thing for years.

When I was diagnosed with triple negative breast cancer and tested positive for a genetic mutation called

"Check 2," I chose to get a double mastectomy and opt-ed out of breast reconstruction. The main reason I made this decision is because I didn't want any more surgeries. I wanted to be done with this journey as soon as possible. In addition, being a fitness instructor and owning my own company doesn't leave a lot of downtime, so the idea of recovering for weeks at a time just didn't seem like a reasonable option. To be honest, I was also a little bitter at my breasts for trying to kill me. I felt betrayed by them and had severed any connection to them in my mind. Opting out of breast reconstruction felt like the best decision for me.

However, when I was presented with this choice I had no idea how much in the minority I would be. I never gave it much thought. I just assumed that others would probably feel the same as me so I wasn't shy about talking about it. The reaction I got from many caring and well-meaning friends was, "Good for you, but I don't think I could ever do that." I remember coming home one night after a dinner out with a good friend where the conversation had turned in this direction. She said her breasts were something she felt confident about and made her feel beautiful, so she couldn't imagine having to get rid of them. I left dinner questioning whether there was something wrong with me for being okay with having a scar instead of breasts. Was I less of a woman? I didn't feel like it on the inside, but maybe I was missing something.

It was then that I had my "a-ha moment". I realized that, as women, we all have certain aspects of our bodies or beings that we feel good about. They are the parts that become part of our identity and we fall back on them when other parts don't feel as good. Being presented with a choice of having to get rid of a prized physical attribute that you have enjoyed and relied on for most of your life it is devastating. I started thinking of the parts of my body I feel good about and felt really sad about the idea of losing them. However, I felt serenity settle in about my decision. As my confidence came flooding back in, I felt like I truly understood.

I am here to tell you that the route my inner compass took me down has only gotten less scary as I have progressed, which eventually led to a really beautiful destination. When I look in the mirror, I see the girl I always wanted to become: a confident, strong, kind, and happy soul with short hair, bright eyes and a smile as big as her abnormally large biceps (which is one of the body parts I would have a very hard time getting rid of).

I have never felt more like a woman.

I define my femininity. Boobs do not.

Trust your inner compass. It won't let you down.

6
Don't try to take things off other people's plates.

When I first got my diagnosis of cancer, my mind immediately went to my family. My ultimate goal was to try to make things as easy and as normal for my husband, Tim, and my two sons. I didn't want my kids to feel the burden of my sickness, and I didn't want Tim to feel like he had to take care of me 24/7. My natural instinct was to protect everyone.

When it came time for my chemo treatments, I assumed that it would be better for everyone if things just continued as normal with our daily schedules. I had a friend who really wanted to go to chemo with me, so I asked her to join me for my first treatment. I'll never forget Tim's face when I told him that my friend was going to come with me. I said it in a nonchalant way simply because I wanted him to know that it was okay, and I didn't want him to feel like he had to take a day off work.

Naively, I expected him to thank me. Instead, he looked like he had been punched in the stomach. Tim is not one to get upset easily. He rolls with everything, but tears actually started streaming down his face. He was upset that I assumed that he wouldn't want to go with me to the first treatment. He told me that he wanted to be there every step of the way, and that I was more important than anything else on his schedule. He was crushed that I did not talk about this with him first. It really stung him.

For a moment, I was aggravated. I didn't quite understand why he was getting so upset. I was honestly just trying to do him a favor. But the more I thought about it, the more I realized that I had done to him what I get so aggravated at others for doing to me: I made a decision for him. I took something off his plate that he wasn't ready to let go of. I assumed he felt one way, when he really felt another. He wanted to be there for me and and by me not asking him, it came across that I did not want him to be there.

I will never forget this moment. It taught me a great lesson. If you are going through a difficult time, the people who love you want to be there for you. I think there may have been a little fear on my part by letting him in on that part of the journey. I didn't want him to see me in that state and make this more upsetting for him than it had to be. I realize now that I was trying to protect myself more than I was protecting him.

It's okay to let people fully in.

It's okay to fall apart in front of the people you care about.

It's okay if the family dynamic you have relied upon for so long falls apart a little bit. If the foundation is solid, nothing will be able to destroy it. Storms may blow in and wreak havoc, but the sun will come out again and you will realize that everything can be put back together. Make sure your family foundation is strong now!

7
Keep the faith.

I believe in God. I'm a Protestant and have a very strong Christian foundation. I was raised in a house where we went to church every Sunday, prayed before and after dinner, and also before we went to bed. I believe in a loving God who breaks down barriers instead of building them up. I also have respect for others who may believe something a little different than me. I'm not one to quote Bible verses or impose my beliefs on other people.

One thing I do have a very hard time with that started gnawing on me even more as I have been on this journey is the word "blessed". To me, it sounds arrogant. I don't believe God bestows "blessings" on some people and not on others.

I remember hearing someone say, "I'm blessed" after their biopsy came back benign. I felt the heat rise in my face as I considered that maybe I was *not* blessed since my tumor turned out to be cancer. To be honest, this has caused me to rebuke well-meaning friends who quote Bible verses in an effort to comfort me and bring me hope. It has actually made me angry at times because it seems like such an easy way to tell someone to "feel better." I hated that I was feeling like this and started to wonder if maybe I was missing something. Maybe I really wasn't blessed! My head was spinning.

But then I got a visit from my minister, Bonnie Steinroeder. She had visited me before, so our conversation was not new. However, she reminded me of something very important: God doesn't necessarily show up in Bible verses or to certain "chosen" ones. He shows up in people. And she reminded me of all the ways God has been present in my life throughout this journey. Bonnie didn't offer me a Bible verse to try to explain why things happen, or give me strength, or try to justify how I should feel. She simply showed up with so much love in her heart and wrapped it around me like a warm blanket.

Then I started to think of all the other special people in my life who have had their hand on my back, making sure I don't stumble and that I keep moving forward. God is surrounding me every day. My frustration and confusion over the word "blessed" has been replaced with a deep appreciation that no matter what happens, God truly has a special place in my heart. Knowing this has helped me get through my diagnosis, surgery, and treatment.

I have a tattoo in my dad's handwriting on the outside of my forearm that says, "Keep the faith." My dad has always instilled the importance of faith in my life and for that I am forever grateful. It's a reminder to me every day to trust that when I feel overwhelmed and out of control, that's the time to take a deep breath and rely on my faith. Believe in something bigger than yourself and try to notice all the ways faith is showing up for you.

8

Adjust your sails and make decisions.

My Morfar was a Danish ship captain. He had tattoos, a deep voice with a heavy Danish accent and was missing a finger on one of his hands. He commanded respect from anyone who came in contact with him. For a kid, that can be a little scary. For many years, the fact that I never felt particularly close to him made me feel that I was missing out on a typical grandfather-granddaughter relationship. But looking back on this now, I realize how much this man's presence in my life taught me, and I am beyond proud that we share the same DNA. In fact, it is this genetic makeup that I believe is pushing me through my current challenge.

There are two very distinct lessons my Morfar taught me. The first involves making decisions. When I was about eight years old, I remember arriving at my Mormor and Morfar's house and my Morfar asking his usual question, "What do you want to drink?" For some reason, on this day I said, "I don't care." My Morfar's head snapped back to glare at me, "Don't you ever say you don't care when someone asks you what you want! Don't give anyone else the power to make a decision for you. You make your own decisions. Now what is it you want to drink?" To be honest, my face flushed a bit with shame because being called out by this man was definitely not comfortable. However, the lesson has stuck with me until this day.

The other lesson I learned from my Morfar is the importance of adjusting your sails — which makes perfect sense coming from a ship captain. After my Mormor passed away, my Morfar was forced to carry on without her. He moved to a retirement home close to us, which was completely out of his element. My Mormor had been the social one, so now my Morfar was left to make new friends in a completely different environment. He never complained or flinched. He just carried on. He dressed up for dinner, wore his signature cologne, and still commanded the same respect from anyone he came in contact with. If he was sad on the inside, we never knew it. Independence and respect was still extremely important to him.

A few years later, my Morfar suffered a debilitating stroke. He lost his ability to speak and stand up and walk. He had to move out of his apartment into an assisted living facility and depended on my mom and dad for most everything in his life. My Morfar lost every sense of the independence and source of strength he had relied upon for his entire life. From the outside looking in, he was a shell of his former self. But the Danish ship captain was still holding on deep within his soul. He never complained. He still made sure my mom kept his hair and nails trimmed, clean and tidy. My Morfar dug deep to remain in control of whatever he possibly could until the very end. He refused to be a victim.

Never let anyone take away your power. Practice building that confidence now. When people ask you what you want, tell them. And when things don't go the way you had planned, turn your sails into the wind and never abandon your ship, just like my Morfar.

9

Get over yourself.

*"I think people don't understand that acceptance is a choice
and sometimes it's a bit of work. Not everything just 'is.'
The mind is a muscle and needs to be worked too."*
— Pam Gibbs

I got this message from an old friend after an incident I had on a very hot summer day. I had gone out for a morning run and it was so hot that I opted out of a hat and wore a tank top. I passed three men on my route. All of them had no problem staring at my bald head from a distance, but as soon as they got next to me, they dropped their eyes and pretended I wasn't there. This only made me yell "GOOD MORNING!" louder.

Truth be told, this whole experience with the physical changes that cancer and chemo have brought my way have been eye-opening. I have never considered myself a vain person, but I, like any other woman, have always liked to feel pretty. Getting compliments about my appearance felt nice. Noticing people staring was always something positive. It's taken me a while to get used to the fact that the stares are now coming from a different perspective. My appearance now can make people uncomfortable. My bald head and flat chest are a scary reminder to people of a very realistic worst-case scenario.

Fortunately, I have a little bit of an "I'll show you" side to my personality which has really served me well over the last couple of months. But I have to be honest. Some days it's really hard.

My friend Pam has a special needs daughter and wanted me to know she could totally relate to this experience. In fact, she told me that she reminds her daughter to say "GOOD MORNING" just as loudly as I do whenever people stare and say nothing. Pam reminded me that things that make people uncomfortable about us are what makes us proud of ourselves. That's on them.

I'm so grateful for my super smart friends who always seem to know just what to say.

Stare all you want, but be kind and *see* people. And for goodness sake, say "Good Morning"! Get over yourself.

10

Find your Belinda.

I'll never forget the day I told my brother I found a lump. It came out as kind of just a casual mention in a conversation we were having about something else over the phone. I downplayed it, but he wouldn't let it go. He asked questions, but in typical Chris fashion, he turned it into something we could laugh at. Laughter comes in handy during scary situations.

Let me back it up a bit and tell you that I was blessed with a third nipple. This has been a constant source of humor for me and my family, and it's now more ironic that even after a double mastectomy, I still have a boob. My brother immediately used his one-of-a-kind humor to spin a wild tale that maybe the third nipple actually belonged to a Siamese twin living inside my body and this "lump" was just her trying to push her way out. The story that unraveled out of my brother's mouth was so hysterically bizarre that I actually had to pull the car over because I was laughing so hard. He kept going. He named my "Siamese twin" *Belinda*. No offense to any Belindas out there. I'm sure you are lovely!

From there, a complete character and storyline was formed. My tumor was personified as a hard-living, selfish, trashy woman from Lowell, MA (no offense to anybody from Lowell) who had a mangy dog that looked like a rat. And it didn't stop there. A rallying social media hashtag was born: "DBB" which stands for "Dat Bitch Belinda".

"DBB" was a way for us to take some of the fear out of a very scary situation. Humor does that. I will forever be grateful for my brother and his wildly hilarious imagination. It has definitely been one of the most helpful gifts I have received along this journey. When given the choice, I will always choose laughing over crying. Make sure you find someone hysterical who will help you find the Belinda in your challenging story line. And if you don't have anyone, do it for yourself.

11

If you see something, say something.

One of the hardest things about this journey is the feeling of being invisible. Maybe *invisible* isn't even the right word, because people *are* looking. It's the looking and then looking away that is so hard on the ego. Deep inside you know that people don't really want to be faced with what you are going through because it's a stark reminder that it could happen to them or someone they love. For others, I think they catch themselves staring and not wanting to be rude, immediately avert their eyes. To be fair, I think people are trying to do the right thing. But from the perspective of the person behind the mask and under the hat, it's brutal.

Some days I feel strong and I can put my blinders on and say I don't care; or better yet, even laugh. But on other days — when it feels as if I'm swimming upstream against a strong current — I want to tear my mask off, rip off my hat, throw my body on the ground, and have a meltdown. It was on a day like this that I walked out of the grocery store, removed my mask and kept my eyes on the ground. I was tired of everything. Sometimes it all just gets to you. A man was walking a few feet ahead of me and made his way to his landscaping truck. He looked just as tired as me. Instead of getting into his truck, he turned in my direction and surprised me. He said, "Keep up the fight. Stay strong. You are beautiful."

I stopped and immediately burst into tears. He looked a little surprised at my reaction, but there was such kindness in his eyes. We both stood there for a moment, neither one of us making any move to come physically closer. It was almost as if we were both just taking in the moment. I'll be honest, I have been told I was beautiful before, but never has that compliment meant so much to me. Despite my mask, my hat, and feeling like such a hollow shell of a human, I felt like my soul was truly being seen.

I truly believe we should seek to discover the souls of the people around us. If we stop being afraid of recognizing pain and hardship in others, we can consider what we can do to make a positive difference in that moment. Cheer someone on with genuine encouragement. You have no idea how one kind word can truly fuel someone whose tank is empty.

12

Do something shocking.

When I was in seventh grade I suffered from crippling anxiety and depression. I had always been a nervous kid, but this particular year the floodgates seemed to open. I was overwhelmed by my fears, lack of self-confidence, and sadness that my world seemed to be changing faster than I wanted it to. I felt completely lost and out of control. I woke up every morning, barely able to eat, with my stomach in knots over having to walk through the doors of school. And every afternoon, I retreated to my room and cried for hours unable to understand why I was feeling the way I was. I stopped smiling and laughing, and slowly became a shell of myself.

I remember moments from this time of my life so vividly that I can actually feel the knots starting to form in my stomach. I desperately want to go back in time and give that Carly a hug and tell her it's going to be okay. But, as hard as that time of my life was for me, I also feel an enormous sense of pride over how I was able to dig deep and develop a fierce inner strength at such a young age to get myself through it. What I learned about myself during that time has truly been what has helped me get through every struggle I have faced since then. There was a defining moment, however, that became the turning point I reflect upon almost daily.

When I started eighth grade, I was doing a little better with my anxiety, but still suffered from a major lack of confidence. I still preferred holding back instead of pushing forward, so when I heard about the student council and the options we had for running for office, my first reaction was to tell myself, "Absolutely not. There is no way I can do that." But for some reason I couldn't stop thinking about it. I felt a fire in my belly and an inner voice telling me that just maybe I could do it. It wasn't just the student council I wanted to be a part of, though. For some reason, I was driven to go for gold. I wanted to be President of the Student Council!

I remember coming home from school and telling my mom I had made the decision to run. The look on her face was initially one of amusement, and then turned to a bit of confusion mixed with apprehension. She asked if I had considered maybe just starting out with being on the council or even something a little lower on the chain of command, like secretary. I told her I had already declared I was running and that there was only one other candidate, which happened to be the most popular girl in school. I was determined, and I believed deep down in my tippy toes that I could win. I'm not sure anyone else was as confident as I was, but regardless, my mom and my friends rallied behind me to create a campaign I will never forget.

I was pushed way out of my comfort zone. I had to redefine myself and convince people that the quiet girl who was lower on the popularity totem pole was the right girl for the job, even though there were moments I wasn't quite sure I was. I based my campaign on kindness and showing people who I really was, making sure I was nice and friendly to everyone. Even at that young age, I was able to use my struggles to relate to people.

I will never forget the feeling of waiting for the results of the election in a classroom with all the other candidates. The winners were read over the loudspeaker. When my name was announced as the eighth-grade class president, all the other people in that room ran over to console the most popular girl in school, but I didn't care. I walked out of that classroom to the cheers of all my classmates and to this day, I don't think I have ever felt so proud of myself.

I think of this moment every day. I truly believe that every single challenge you go through in life sets you up for the next one. If you don't stop and reflect, it's easy to miss the lesson and undervalue the growth that comes with getting over each hurdle. Some challenges you choose and some you don't. It's important to have a mix because they are equally as important in your growth as a human being who can handle hard things.

13

Lend strength when you can.

Recently I had a conversation with one of my mom's good friends, Jane, who tragically lost her husband over a decade ago. She told me about a woman she had recently become friends with who didn't know the story about her husband, until she asked Jane if she was divorced. Jane filled her in on the story about her husband's death. The woman was so moved that the next day she left a sweet card and a lovely bouquet of flowers on Jane's porch. Jane said that no matter how much time passes, those surprising gestures of kindness and care still mean so much.

We also talked a bit about people who surprise us in the opposite way. Sometimes it's hard to understand why some of the people we think care so much about us, seem to retreat into the darkness instead of taking a step forward. We both agreed that some of it may have to do with fear. It's not easy coming face to face with a tragedy that could happen to you. It can bring up a lot and sometimes the easier thing to do is to tell yourself the person who is suffering has plenty of other people who care, so it really doesn't matter if you extend yourself or not.

I am here to tell you that it *does* matter.

If you have a friendship or relationship with another human being and you value it, it's essential you put your fear aside and step up to take their hand during a challenging time. If you are scared and having a tough time dealing with the situation, it's imperative you communicate that to the person.

There are many ways of lending support. You don't have to make a meal, send a gift, or show up on their doorstep. A simple text or call to check in will do. You don't even have to wait for a response. Simply saying "I'm thinking of you" can make a world of difference to someone who is struggling. It's a metaphorical way of gently placing your hand on someone's back to keep them from falling down. You have no idea how that kind of support infuses a person's soul with strength.

I'm going to be very blunt here. If you value someone in your life and would like to continue your relationship or friendship after the storm passes, get over yourself and *show up*. If you don't, be prepared for that friendship to be over. One of the greatest blessings of going through a tough time is to see human kindness at its purest level and to realize who your true friends are.

14

Make your mess your masterpiece.

There is a lot of power that can be found in your weakest moments.

Believe it or not, I have felt the strongest on my sickest days. There is something very powerful that happens when you know you are down for the count, but you still manage to fight and overcome whatever it is that's ailing you. On those days, my anxiety has stayed at bay because my energy is consumed with just getting through the day.

It's when my body started to feel better and back to normal that I struggled most. That's when I started absolutely dreading having to go back to Dana Farber. It's right about that time that I started gagging at the thought of chewing on LifeSavers and peppermints to alleviate the anti-nausea medicine taste as it's going into my port and dry heaving at the idea of having to chew ice to prevent mouth sores as the "red devil" is being injected into my body.

But, lucky for me, and knowing how I tend to react to things, I thought ahead before this process even started. I wracked my brain for a way to give some purpose to and shine some light on an annoying and inevitable situation.

So I started the "Chemo Coffee Talk Podcast" straight from my chemo chair!

This idea has given me a place to send my thoughts when the dread starts creeping in. My brain calms down when I start thinking about the special "Chemo Buddy" I will be interviewing and getting to spend some quality time with.

It's truly the best idea I ever had.

We all go through things in life that are extremely unpleasant and hard to take. These times can often break you down to depths you never even knew existed and leave you questioning if you can handle it. It's in these moments that you can sometimes find your greatest strength.

The ball is in your court. Think outside the box. Make your mess your masterpiece.

Pray for the bear.

15

Sunday Spotlights on My Chemo Buddies

Back in 2019 I was scrolling on Instagram and started to get really annoyed at how so many ridiculous people seemed to be famous, getting recognition for absolutely nothing positive. I started to think about all the fabulous and inspiring people I was so grateful to have in my life and how a lot of them go unnoticed. I wanted a way to highlight them and let them know what a major impact they have had on my life. So every Sunday I started posting a "Sunday Spotlight" on Facebook celebrating the awesomeness of someone in my life.

To be honest, the people I choose kind of choose me! If I can't write about them in ten minutes, I know it's not the right time to highlight them. Many times the people I have showcased have reached out to me and asked how I seemed to know exactly what they needed to hear right at that moment. To me, that is the greatest thing I could hear.

I thought I would dig into my Sunday Spotlight archives and share the posts I wrote about my "Chemo

Buddies." I didn't realize until writing this book that every single one of them had been featured at one time throughout the years. I guess it kind of makes sense. So if you haven't listened to "Chemo Coffee Talk" here is a glimpse of the wonderful souls who joined me in my studio/infusion room:

TIM

"Tougher Than the Rest" is my favorite Bruce Springsteen song. It's not only the spot-on lyrics, it's also the steady beat, Bruce's comforting "Jersey Shore" accent, and the fact that it's not a big production. It doesn't need to show off with an epic guitar jam or an earth-shattering saxophone solo to make its statement. It's subtle yet unforgettable. The other day I realized I love this song so much because it reminds me of my husband, Tim.

Tim is the type of guy who will walk the line for you again and again and again and never ask or expect you to do it for him in return. He's the type of guy that will pick up your pieces if you fall apart and stay right by your side to help you put them back together. And his quick-witted humor and "glass half full" attitude won't allow you to take the situation or yourself too seriously. Tim always celebrates the success of others, but often stays quiet about his own because there is no need to flaunt something that can speak for itself. He's humble and kind and fiercely devoted to those he loves. It takes a strong character to journey through life by my side. If I were him, I probably would have thrown in the towel a long time ago, but not Tim. He has a subtle way of keeping me in line while letting me be me and loving me for exactly who I am. No matter how tough I get, he always makes me feel like I'm the only girl in the room. He's my steady beat...with that same comforting Jersey Shore accent Bruce has. Be kind. Be humble. Keep your sense of humor. Be tougher than the rest. Be like Tim.

BRENDA

Her house is white… the rugs, the couches, the pillows. Everything. When she first told me about this, I legitimately felt the beginning of a panic attack at the prospect of keeping all of that clean… but then I reminded myself, this is Brenda Chiaradonna! She is a woman with impeccable style who always seems to be perfectly and effortlessly dressed. And her style extends beyond just fashion. She transforms the interiors of homes into things you never thought possible. Her attention to detail is awe inspiring and could easily be intimidating to those of us not quite as "stylishly gifted."

But here is the thing that makes Brenda amazing: she invites you to her white house and doesn't require you to remove your shoes. She genuinely wants you to feel comfortable. She doesn't freak out when your kids are running through her living room. She doesn't have one eye on everyone making sure their hands are clean and nothing is spilling, and when her friend asks if she can tape a poster to the perfect wall in her impeccable living room for a game for the kids, she says, "Of course". When I asked her about how she can be so laid back about people possibly ruining all her nice white things she said, "Carly, *everything* is fixable."

It was then that I realized that Brenda's style is so much more than just the beautiful visual stuff she puts together. It's a stunning, warm and welcoming feeling she creates as well. It comes from her soul, and that truly makes her one of the coolest and most talented people I've ever met. Be real. Create beautiful things and feelings. Keep things in perspective. Remember everything is fixable... be like Brenda.

Colleen

When I ask her to bike 40 miles with me on an early Sunday morning, she enthusiastically says yes and enjoys every wind in the road as much as I do. When I tell her I'm doing a burpee challenge, she says, "Awesome! Can I join in?" When I invite her to a party at my house where she won't know anyone, she says, "Can't wait! What can I bring?" When I'm feeling really frustrated, sad, or upset, she listens, lets me cry, and then suggests meeting for a beer. She cheers for my boys as loudly as I do and offers her own absolutely amazing kids to take care of them when I need some help. She's friends with my husband and always cheers for him, too.

At 42 years old, I never thought I would have a playmate who brings that same kind of unbridled joy I felt when I was a little kid playing with my best friends. Colleen has taught me that, "Growing old is mandatory. Growing up is optional." And for that, among many other things, I'm so grateful for her.

AMANDA

I watched the series finale of "Ted Lasso" last night. I had been putting it off because I didn't want it to actually be over. Saying goodbye to characters on a show that I love is heartbreaking for me and it usually takes me weeks to recover from it.

I was surprisingly able to keep my composure until nearly the end. The "Believe" sign scene got me. And it wasn't just because of the meaning of the scene within the show, and how it related to each of the characters. I started getting teary because I thought of my friend Amanda. I had seen her earlier in the week right after she finished watching the episode and her eyes were still filled with tears. She assured me it was a happy ending, but she just had a lot going on and her tears were a culmination of all of it. Perhaps that's why she popped into my head during this scene.

Amanda is one of those strong types of humans that

has had a lot of challenges placed in her path. Those circumstances could easily derail someone. But not Amanda. She has this unique inner strength and belief in herself that fuels her to rise up and keep going no matter who or what tries to pull down her "Believe" sign. She is always able to grab the tape to fix it and get it back up where she can focus on it. But what's even more remarkable about Amanda is that when your "Believe" sign may start falling down or get a couple of tears, she's consistently there to help you mend it.

Don't let anyone or anything ever take your "Believe" sign down. Keep repairing it and stick it back up there where you can see it. And remember to lend your tape to someone else. Be like my friend Amanda.

Lisa C.

I have been extremely fortunate with those who have been placed in the path of my life. Some of these people have been placed there to wrap their arms around me, some have been put there to soften my edges or teach me a life lesson. And then there is Lisa C.

The funny thing about meeting Lisa is that at the outset, the purpose of our getting to know each other was me helping her. I had absolutely no idea of the impact she would have on me. This woman is proof that if you want something bad enough, and you are willing to work hard, you can have it. Lisa will not allow anyone or anything to block her path. And if she falls down, she doesn't point fingers and play the blame game. As uncomfortable as it may be, she owns her defeats and rises back up twice as strong. And she expects nothing less from others.

Lisa will not allow you to get lost in the haze of self-doubt. She'll grab your hand, give you a swift kick in the pants and guide you back to clarity about who you are and what you can accomplish. She's a true cheerleader. Lisa takes no excuses and makes no excuses and that's one of the ten thousand reasons I think she is so absolutely awesome. Be your best self and remind others to be their best too. Be like Lisa.

Lynn

My first personal interaction with Lynn Canty was about ten years ago when she came back for a second time to one of my Tabata classes. I asked her with my overwhelming enthusiasm, "Lynn!! Aren't you so excited for Tabata??" Her response didn't involve any words. She just looked up and gave me the absolute *best* side eye I have ever seen in my life. She came back the next week, gave me the same legendary look, but in the next breath declared Q-Tip's "Vivrant Thing" my theme song, and then actually gave me a sly smile! It was right at that moment that I realized I wanted to be friends with Lynn Canty forever.

Since then, I have developed a friendship with Lynn that actually surpasses the high expectations I had when we first met. Lynn is the type of friend who truly listens and always seems to be able to make perfect and eloquent sense of anything that may be stumping me. Her dry and smart sense of humor often leaves me in belly laughs, and for the rest of the day I'm starting sentences like, "To quote my friend, Lynn Canty..."

But, the thing I respect most about Lynn is that she's able to perfectly balance privacy and openness. She's willing to share things about herself, but only what's relevant. She never makes a conversation focused on herself, or seeks attention. Her conversation style is kind and generous, just like her soul. Lynn is an expert at downplaying her awesomeness. It's that quality that always makes you want to know a little bit more about her, but you don't ask. Because if you do, you're going to get that legendary Lynn Canty side eye.

Katelyn

There is a very fine line between sarcasm and support, and I don't think I have ever met anyone that toes the line quite as perfectly as Katelyn. She's the type of friend who will give you an honest answer, but say it in such a way that it will make you laugh at yourself. Then she'll linger long enough to make sure you know that she gets you and you're not alone. She can dish it out, but she can also take it like a champ. Katelyn is the type of person who supports you, subtly, simply by showing up, consistently. She's the type of girl who says *Yes* to a triathlon group you start and then is the only member to show up to the actual race *on her birthday*, on a busted bike which ends up breaking during the race causing a bloody injury. But she still has the sense of humor to take it all in stride and laugh it off, all the while telling you how she will never forget how you forced her to join your *#%^*#+ stupid Triathlon group*. Katelyn's friendship reminds me not to take myself so seriously and that life is *way* more fun when you can laugh at yourself and invite others to join in with you.

BROOKE

I just found this picture and I immediately thought to myself, "How on earth has she not been my Sunday Spotlight!?" And then I smirked and thought, "Well, because she would probably roll her eyes!" That's Brooke. That's the girl who has ALL the dirt on me. That's my ride or die, the friend who understands where I'm coming from, without me having to explain. She's the one who has always had the ability to call me out, but will be the first person to stand next to me when I need her by my side. Brooke is the one who will proudly wear a dress I made for her in a college costume construction class (It's beautiful isn't it?) to a Christmas party because she thinks "it's cool and who the hell cares?" She is the one that will make you fabulous playlists that serenade your sadness and then give you some kick ass lyrics to build you back up from really bad boyfriends. Brooke is the friend who will bond with your husband and the one who will make an effort to hold on and steady the ship even when it feels like your friendship may be sinking. She never gives up. No matter how cynical she may seem or how much time passes in between talking or seeing each other, Brooke is that rock solid friend who has stood the test of time. Hold on to those special friendships. Be a ride or die. Be like Brooke.

CHRIS

This Spotlight has been on my mind for a while, but it's taken me a little time to cut it down to a reasonable length. If you are lucky enough to know my brother, chances are at some point you've said to yourself or out loud, "Oh that Chris Nyland!" Growing up, he was forgetful, messy and disorganized. He was teased by his classmates and even sometimes by his teachers. But he was (and still is), incredibly forgiving, hilariously funny, kindhearted and sweet.

In high school, it wasn't uncommon for him to show up in a class and then realize he was a couple periods too early. He forgot his lunch on a daily basis (good thing he had a sister who always packed a little extra) and on some days he forgot his entire backpack. No matter how much we all tried to help him, he couldn't seem to pull it together. He ended up reluctantly going to community college and that is where one day it just finally clicked.

Long story short, he finally woke up and paid attention. His incredible focus and determination to study hard led to his acceptance to UNH, where he absorbed every single second of his experience and found things he was really good at. He didn't stop there either. He went on to get his master's from the University of Miami. He's married now, has two amazing kids, a great job and kicks some serious ass every day of his life.

He still struggles at times, like we all do. But that's when I see that determination shine through again and again, and I sit back in such awe. And he's still one of the nicest, most hilarious humans around. "Oh that Chris Nyland!" Turn your struggles into fuel. Fight back. Believe in yourself. Never give up. Be kind. Be like my hero. Be like Chris.

Christie

One of the first times I met Christie, she walked into my class with some very oddly colored and severe eyebrows. I wasn't sure if I should say something, but I was a little puzzled by her look. We chatted for a bit and then she talked to some other people coming in, who all gave her the same curious look.

When she finally turned to look in the mirror in the

Barre room, she let out a hysterical scream and proceeded to fall to the ground laughing to the point of tears. Apparently she had just gotten her eyebrows waxed and forgotten to rub off the shaping marks, and she had been walking around town like that all morning.

I don't think I have ever seen someone laugh so hard at themselves and invite others to join in. That's Christie in a nutshell. Her sense of humor and warm honesty make even the saddest, scariest or plain old yuckiest situations seem bearable. Self-deprecating humor can be a form of therapy, especially in a world where we tend to take ourselves so seriously. Christie will help you laugh so hard at yourself that you will pee your pants, and then she'll be the first person to offer to bring you a clean pair and also throw in a jar of her homemade pickles and honey because she knows how much you love them. She's a good egg. And it's hard for me to imagine what my life was like before she entered it.

SHEILA

Simply put, Sheila is one of my favorite human beings. She's one of my best friends, and I could go on and on about what she means to me. But that's not why she is my Sunday Spotlight. I want to give Sheila a shout out for her friendship with someone else. Let me preface this by saying that Sheila is one of the hardest working people I've ever known. She and her husband work extremely hard, oftentimes putting in very long hours, to provide for their family. Life is crazy and free time is scarce.

A few years ago, Sheila's closest friend was diagnosed with cancer. Throughout her battle, Sheila was by her side every step of the way. Last year, Sheila's friend was told she needed a liver transplant and had to travel across the country to a special hospital to get the surgery. Without missing a beat, Sheila dropped everything, bought herself a one-way ticket (she was prepared to stay as long as needed) and flew out to help her friend recover from the surgery. She moved into the hospital room and literally nursed her friend back to being healthy enough to travel back with her.

When I told Sheila how amazing she was for doing this, she brushed it off and looked me right in the eye and said "I would do the same thing for you, Cod!" And I can honestly say I believe her. There are 1,000,000 reasons why I love this girl. But there is one thing that sets Sheila apart from a lot of other people. For the best parts of your life and the worst parts of your life, Sheila always shows up. I love you, Sheila.

CARISSA

Pay attention. When you meet someone for the first time and it seems like you have very little in common, but you hear a little voice in your head telling you this person is someone special, *listen*. Lifelong friendships can develop when you least expect it.

Carissa can wear white pants, a crisp white shirt and keep herself gleaming for the entire day. When I wear white, I immediately end up sitting in chocolate or spilling whatever I'm eating on my shirt. Carissa accessorizes with understated, yet classic and fabulous jewelry. I wear earrings from Target. I love to jump around and sweat my face off. When I first met Carissa she didn't own a pair of sneakers (but she does now!).

But here's the thing: for all our differences, we have always been each other's biggest fans. We cheer for each other and celebrate all the things that make both of us who we are. And when one of us is down, we rush in to help the other up. We can go months without talking or seeing each other because in this kind of friendship, the roots are so strong you can just pick up where you left off. Take notice of the people who are put in your path. Celebrate what each of you bring to the table. "Differences allow us to be fascinated by each other."

Lisa F.

If you knew me when I was a little girl, you know exactly who the blonde girl with the pigtails is peeking over my shoulder. Lisa. My childhood best friend who was present in all childhood memories since birth. She lived across the street from me until we moved across town, but that didn't have any effect on our bond. Her parents are Norwegian and since my family is Danish we thought our friendship was totally meant to be. We agreed it was and more special than anyone else's because we both had "Mormors" (grandmothers) and we both could say "Jeg elsker dig" (I love you) being that it's said the same in Norwegian and Danish.

We always talked about the fact that we would be friends forever and neither one of us could ever imagine life without the other. We made the absolute best memories together extending beyond childhood into our early adulthood. We spent so many years happily journeying down the same path, side by side.

But life happens. And for whatever reason, due to nobody's fault, signals got crossed and distances widened. Somewhere along the line, we took separate turns on that path and it became difficult to find each other. Thinking about it would make me sad and looking at this picture always made me wonder if maybe I was glorifying the memories and maybe the friendship I had always held so close to my heart wasn't as special and as true as I once thought it was. Maybe those years and that friendship wasn't as special to her as it was to me.

And then a month ago I received a package in the mail. It was "The Hygge Game," a Danish-themed cozy conversation starter card game. And the card in the package read:

"Hi Carly. I saw this game and of course thought of

you. Jeg elsker dig! — Lisa"

My eyes instantly watered and my heart melted. It was then that I realized no matter how much time goes by or how much distance grows, the memories and love that are created in a true friendship never go away.

Reach out and tell someone you remember. No matter how much time has passed or the distance that has grown between you, reassure them that the memories are important and the times you spent together mean something to you. Do what Lisa did.

16

Trust the process.

Getting a cancer diagnosis is truly one of the scariest moments I have ever had to go through. But I will tell you that it's not just hearing "You have cancer," that sends shivers down your spine. The absolute most horrifying part is navigating the red tape to make sure you have assembled the best team possible for you.

Unfortunately for many of us, insurance plays a big role in this decision. Sometimes the teams and doctors you've heard rave reviews about are not in your insurance network. I spent days in a complete panic and shed many tears while trying to navigate our healthcare system. It seemed like every time I turned around, someone else was telling me about a life changing experience they had with a certain surgeon, hospital or oncologist, and I immediately felt the urgency to check out every single one of them. When your life's on the line, you don't want to leave any stone unturned. I look back on this aspect of my journey as the most mentally and emotionally exhausting part of the process.

The insurance-approved surgeon I was referred to

was not on any of the "Dream Team" lists I received from friends, and friends of friends, who had battled breast cancer in my area. In fact, she wasn't even affiliated with any of the top hospitals, but I kept the appointment simply because I didn't know what else to do. Looking back, I'm so happy I did.

As soon as Dr. Dinh walked into the room on the day of my appointment, I felt a sense of calm. Although I didn't know much about her, there was some kind of divine energy she put out that meshed perfectly with mine. She didn't have the arrogant attitude that some surgeons have. She was young. She was a mom. She understood.

After our meeting, I went home and did a little research and sent some emails to other doctors I know, and all I received were glowing reports about Dr. Dinh and her care. I felt confident she was the surgeon for me. I was able to set all my Boston hospital surgeon research aside and fully put my trust in Dr. Dinh and Milford Hospital.

I'm forever grateful to Dr. Dinh for the way she handled my surgery and the incredible job she did taking me apart and putting me back together. My entire surgery team was female, and I felt like Dr. Dinh was a true captain. Since my surgery was done at the hospital in my town, I had the pleasure of one of the anesthesiologist nurses being my friend. She offered to lead my team, and it was so comforting to know her face would be the last one I saw before going out (thank you Tricia!). Because of my amazing team, I look back on surgery day with fond memories and absolutely no fear associated with it.

The next part of my cancer team is my oncologist. I did my research on this as well, and the name I kept hearing in response to my questions was "Dr. Sinclair." Even the top surgeons and oncologists in Boston told me there was no need to travel into Boston when I had Dr. Sinclair available right outside my back door at Dana Farber. Luckily for me, I have a dear friend who is a patient of Dr. Sinclair's. She went into her appointment soon after my diagnosis and tearfully begged Dr. Sinclair to take me on.

I have never in my entire life met a care provider like Dr. Sinclair. Her bedside manner is kind and understanding. She's quick to laugh and eager to do whatever she can to help ease the awful journey she knows you are on. She's also a fierce advocate for her patients and will go to bat for them and fight for what she knows they need. I put all my faith in her and let her know I would do anything she said was the best way for me to get this cancer out of my body and make sure it never comes back. Dr. Sinclair is a huge reason why I have been able to truly believe deep down in my tippy-toes that I will beat this. Without her, I'm not sure my journey would look the way it does.

The third, and probably the most personal part of my cancer team is my chemo nurse, Lauren. For those of you who don't know, usually you are paired with a chemo nurse who stays with you throughout your entire course of treatment. You develop an intimate relationship with your chemo nurse, a relationship that's a bit hard to understand unless you have been through it. Your chemo nurse is the one you are trusting to inject the poison into your body, and you both know it's going to make you feel really sick. That bond alone is something you most likely will never experience with anyone else.

Lauren was not supposed to be my chemo nurse. I was told it was going to be someone else, but there was a change made at the last minute. When she walked in, I was a little unsure because she looked way too young to be fully trusted. However, my naïve lack of confidence was soon replaced with nothing but indescribable admiration and unbelievable gratitude. Since day one, Lauren has played along with all my slightly over-the-top antics. She's laughed at my wigs, championed my podcast, and been a guest. She has chuckled along with my chemo buddies and even makes sure to ask about how they are doing. Lauren knows I need things written down and sends Instagram messages me to remind me.

The decision-making process during cancer or any health crisis can be absolutely terrifying and overwhelming. Try to keep your wits about you. Ask questions. Do your research, but also tune into your gut. Control what you can, but have the courage to trust that you will be led in the right direction and that the team that comes together will be the right one for you.

17

Action leads to motivation.

My husband and I are not independently wealthy, so we have always relied on my income as well as his. I have always had some kind of full-time job, but really developed a solid side hustle with my passion for fitness. In May 2023, I finally got up enough courage to make my fitness side hustle my full-time job. Starting my own company was something I never thought I could do. I think I always had a fear that if I turned it into something legitimate, it would take the fun out of it. And what if I failed? But, after some deep soul searching and reflection, I finally built up enough confidence in myself to take the leap.

I developed the **FitFunCarly Method** and created an entire fitness community around it called the **FITFUN-COMMUNITY**. My method is based on the fact that consistency and joy are the two most important factors when it comes to developing a healthy and realistic relationship with fitness. My platform provides a diverse collection of live 15-minute workouts each day, along with some longer format workouts as well. Everything is also available On Demand. I have found that everyone has time for 15 minutes of movement during their day. It's a great place to develop a healthy habit or to add on a little extra to what you may already be doing.

Just when I felt like I was really building momentum with the business, life threw me one of infamous curve balls. Mine came in the form of my breast cancer diagnosis in February of 2024. I remember thinking to myself, "Cancer and a fitness business are a terrible combination. How could this possibly work?"

Little did I know, my very own method and my **FIT-FUNCOMMUNITY** would truly end up saving me.

My **FITFUNCOMMUNITY** members were the first people I told about my diagnosis. While I was open and honest with them in sharing my fears about the future, I promised them I was committed to showing up for them, no matter what that might look like. The love and support I received from them still blows my mind. They have stood by me in such a powerful way, even volunteering to come to my house after my double mastectomy surgery to be my body double so I could still teach while I was recovering. The love I have received from them brings me to tears. There is no way I could have made it through this and kept my business afloat without them.

The other way I have been saved is using the **FitFun-Carly** method itself. I used my own 15-minute workouts to ease myself back into exercise after my double mastectomy. Doing my own classes allowed me to work on my strength and cardio in a safe and practical way. I truly believe that is what helped me heal so fast from my surgery. Even my surgeon was amazed at how quickly I bounced back.

This has only continued during chemo. Knowing that I have made a commitment to show up for the members of my **FitFunCommunity** each day has been a driving force in what has kept me so mentally and physically strong. My goal has been to move at least 15 minutes a day, and my format has helped me reach that goal every single day. No matter what I feel like when I start, I *always* feel better physically and mentally after I move.

I get a lot of messages from people asking me how I get myself motivated to move every day when I am feeling so sick. The truth is, I don't think about *what* it is that I'm going to do. If I did that, I may not do it. Instead, I rely on the healthy fitness habit that I have created for myself. My mind immediately goes to how great I'm going to feel when I'm done. I've learned this from experience. That's what keeps me going. That's where the motivation comes from.

There is absolutely nothing that makes me any different from anyone else. I'm not an Olympic athlete, and I don't have any superpowers. All I have is a strong belief that movement and community are medicine, and I will do anything to make myself feel better. You have that power, too. You just need to take action to unleash it.

18

Learn the secret to staying fit – and the true meaning of fitness.

I had a really good conversation with someone today about "results." She pointed out, and rightfully so, that people are moved to sign up for a fitness program mostly by seeing the physical results of someone who is a part of or has finished that program.

Why Physical Results Matter

People want to actually see the inches lost, the six-pack abs, the bulging biceps, the defined quads and the reduction of the number on the scale. They are interested in knowing the increase in speed and how much more weight can be loaded onto the barbell now compared to when the fitness program began. They want to be able to see what will happen to them *physically* if they decide to sign on for whatever it is being offered.

I can totally understand that. That stuff *is* important. Physical transformation is a huge aspect of why we dedicate ourselves to exercising. It's important to be able to see, feel and recognize how far we have come and the progress we have made towards reaching our goals.

Numerical measurements are the tools we can use to actually see that. They are proof that our hard work is paying off, but they can also be crippling if they are your *only* motivation. Similar to when you are building a house, no matter how beautiful the exterior is, the walls will most likely crumble if the foundation is weak. What I have come to realize over the years, through my own personal fitness journey and helping others along theirs, is that some of the biggest and most beautiful and impressive transformations occur under the surface, at the foundation of who we are.

The Hidden Strength of a Strong Foundation

There are no numerical measurements to gauge this level of internal accomplishment. It doesn't present itself in a flashy Instagram photo or pop out in a Reel. It's not something that can be shown off on a billboard or illustrated in a jaw dropping before and after photo on Facebook. This transformation is not enhanced by a perfectly fitting pair of jeans or a drop-dead pair of shoes. If you look carefully, though, you will be able to see the results shining off these fabulously fit souls.

Spotting the Real Transformations

You will see this transformation in the woman who smiles every morning as she's running up a hill or the lady who walks your block every day at 5:00 pm and always gives you a warm wave.

You will see this in the woman at the pool who shows up every morning to swim and has long since let go of the insecurity of walking around in public in a bathing suit.

You will see this in the girl at your yoga class who has worked really hard to improve her flexibility by making sure to make the 9:00a.m. class every Tuesday and always seems to bring the sunshine in with her.

You will see this in the boy who, despite suffering some serious health setbacks, shows up in your driveway every Thursday with a smile on his face, ready to tackle whatever physical challenge you throw at him.

You will see it in the woman who fought her way back from cancer and started her workouts barely being able to jog in place, but after months of hard work and determination can now burpee with the best of 'em, a twinkle in her eye!

You will see this in the family who shows up to the soccer field at the park every Saturday morning, laughing as they pass the ball and challenge each other to some fancy footwork.

You will see this in the man who gets up at 5:00 am every Sunday to take his morning bike ride and stops for a hot cup of coffee at his favorite cafe.

And you will see this in the happy mother and daughter you meet at the top of the mountain in New

Hampshire, who are on a quest to climb all the peaks in the Presidential Range.

Joy: The Key to Sustainable Fitness

I'll be honest, some of these people may actually have washboard abs and glutes of steel and could easily flaunt themselves on TikTok. And a lot of these people may actually measure their results by the number on a scale, a tape measure or a watch, but it will never exceed the most important thing they have discovered in themselves and placed as the foundation of their fitness journey: **Joy**.

Joy is what keeps them coming back. Joy is the reason for their consistency. Joy is the reason they *feel* the results of their healthy lifestyle and are able to spread that in a much more meaningful way than if it was presented in a picture on social media.

Joy is contagious. The physical transformation will be much more enjoyable and sustainable if we all start with **Joy** and build from there.

19

Stay in **your** moment.

I had a really good conversation with my acupuncturist yesterday.

I was trying to describe the feelings I've been having lately. I seem to be caught in this weird head space that's a concoction of panic and guilt. I think it's because this whole situation has scared the crap out of me.

For years I could hear stories about people struggling with a diagnosis, but then distract my mind and remind myself it wasn't happening to me so it was okay to push that worry out of my mind.

But now I've come face to face with one of my biggest fears.

I'm scared because I now realize this is going to be a part of my life and I'm going to have to find a way to deal with the fear of this happening again to me — or worse, to someone I love. I feel guilty when I hear familiar stories that hit too close to home and wonder why it wasn't me who has to deal with more extreme circumstances.

My acupuncturist asked me to think about all the

challenges I have faced up until this point. She told me *not* to discredit them. She reminded me that they are all part of my own specific journey and have built me up to be able to deal with what I'm going through now. For me to be sitting here worrying about worst case scenarios or feeling guilty comparing my set of challenges to someone else's isn't practicing self-kindness. It's not a good use of my time and energy.

Life is hard. For everyone. Instead of sitting around waiting for the other shoe to drop or obsessively comparing your struggles to someone else's, reflect on the challenges that have built you. Acknowledge them. Be proud of your journey. Take a deep breath.

Stay in **your** moment.

20
Clean out your Rolodex.

They say that the darker the sky, the brighter the stars. I reflect on this quote every time I think of all the wonderful people who have shown up for me during my darkest hours. People have shown up in so many different and wonderful ways. Some have dropped off dinners, others have sent thoughtful gifts and inspiring cards, many have texted, called or emailed just to make sure I know I'm being thought of. There are acquaintances who have taken such a step forward into my life that they have turned into friends whom I know will be in my life forever. These people are true gifts and are a huge reason I have been able to stay so strong.

On the other hand, there are some stars which seem to have either fallen out of the sky or completely lost their glow. While I once thought that some of these stars were the shiniest of all, I now realize that I never actually saw them in contrast to the night sky. After all, everything looks shiny and nice in the sun!

While it can hurt to realize certain friendships and relationships are *not* meant to stand the test of time, it can also be a great time to clean out your Rolodex. For those of you who may be too young to know what exactly a Rolodex is, think of the contacts in your cell phone all written down on little cards and organized in alphabetical order in a circular binder that can easily be flipped through. As I'm sure you can imagine, the Rolodex gets harder to manage and flip through as more names are added. It can get confusing to find the contacts you really need!

Truth be told, life's challenges can end up adding so many new and wonderful names to your Rolodex, so it's actually necessary to make room for them by weeding some names out. Don't get too upset by those who let you down. Their reaction, or lack of, says more about them than it does about you. Focus on all the wonderful people who show up in your life.

Taking out the contacts that are no longer relevant can help you stay more organized and get a better understanding of who exactly is in your network so you can pay more attention to them. Those people deserve your care and concern!

21
Let people help you.

A few weeks before my double mastectomy, my friends Amanda and Karen reached out to me and let me know that they wanted to set up a meal train for me. My first reaction was, "Thank you, but we'll be fine." If I didn't mention this before, I will now: I hate asking for help. I am the type of person who doesn't want to burden other people with my problems. It makes me very uncomfortable to think of someone else having to take time out of their busy schedule to assist me. I have a mindset that I can handle anything on my own.

But the real reason I don't want to ask for help is because I don't want to appear weak.

My friends, Amanda and Karen, lovingly pointed that out to me as I was hemming and hawing at their insistence that having people deliver meals a few times a week would be extremely helpful to me and my family. Because I fully trust them, coupled with the fact that Amanda had been through exactly the same thing as me, I finally said yes.

Once I agreed, Amanda sat me down and gave me

some of the best advice, which I now love to pass along to others. Amanda told me to be direct and very clear with what exactly would be helpful to me and what would not. She began by asking me if I wanted a freezer full of lasagnas and cookies. When I rolled my eyes and scrunched my nose, she said, "Exactly." And then told me to write down the types of foods we liked and didn't like. She also made it very clear we didn't want extra after I told her throwing away food or having lots of uneaten leftovers in my fridge gave me anxiety. She went on by specifying how and when to drop the food off and even went as far as asking for takeout places we liked in case someone wanted to go that route.

I remember the panic starting to set in, worried that people were going to think I was ungrateful and a bit of a snob. Maybe it was too much work for people and nobody would sign up. I felt embarrassed.

Amanda, in her no-nonsense and very direct tone, said to me, "Carly, people want to help you, and the vast majority don't know what you need or what they should do. You are giving them a very clear and easy to understand way of truly doing something that will lessen your burden during this challenging time. In a way, you are giving them a gift by letting them give you a gift. It makes people feel good to help. And you will remember this and pay it forward when the time comes."

I will never forget that message. I will also always

remember every single meal that was dropped off at my house with such love and attention to detail. Nobody thought I was snotty (at least I don't think they did) or resented the extra bit of work it took to make and drop off the meal, and I don't believe anyone thought I was weak either.

Being able to ask for and receive help is a sign of strength. It's also a great way to take part in and absorb one of the most wonderful aspects of being a human being: human kindness. Giving and receiving love and support is the best way we can be there for one another. It not only makes us stronger individually, but it also empowers us as a community!

22
The kids are alright.

When I got the dreaded call from the doctor with my biopsy results, my older son, Ryker, was fourteen years old and had just gotten home from school. My nine-year-old, Kai, was just walking through the door with his best friend. Ryker knew what the call was about. We had given him some details about what was happening, but he didn't know everything. I will forever be grateful to Ryker for ushering Kai and his friend into the other room and giving me the privacy to hear the news by myself. I don't remember much about the phone call, but I do remember taking a few deep breaths to answer my bedroom door when Ryker knocked a couple of minutes later.

Our eyes locked and I told him I had cancer. I could see the confusion in his eyes and his immediate response was to tell me that there was no way he could go to soccer practice after hearing news like this and started to question whether he would again.

I immediately stopped him and made him promise me that whatever journey this ended up looking like, he would never let it take him off the path he was on towards reaching his goals. In other words, he would never be missing a practice on account of me! I also promised him that we would never keep any secrets from him. He would know whatever we knew. In return, I promised him that I would beat this.

From that moment on, Ryker has been dealing with this in his own very special "Ryker" way. He doesn't like to talk about it often, but will on his own terms. He doesn't want special treatment and too much kindness and sensitivity towards him will only make the walls thicken. We have let him take the lead. Sometimes I get frustrated at his seeming lack of sensitivity or lack of interest in what exactly is happening to me, but I know that's part of his defense mechanism. He knows that if he thinks too much about it, he risks losing control of his emotions. When you're fourteen, things are hard enough!

My son, Kai, on the other hand, asks a lot of questions. We handled the situation the same with him and made the same promise of not keeping anything from him. We also let him know it was perfectly fine to be scared, angry and sad, and it always helps to let those feelings out.

Kai has asked numerous times if I am going to die. It's always in a very matter-of-fact way, and as soon as I say no, he is able to continue on with his day. He can read the room better than most adults I know and always seems to understand exactly when I need a hug, kiss or simply a kind word. He likes to ask me exactly how I'm feeling and honestly tries to make comparisons to pain he has experienced in his nine years. It's sweet. And I don't know what I would do without that kind of support.

When this whole thing went down, my biggest fear was how this was going to affect my kids. If you are a mom in a similar situation, I can pretty much guarantee the same thoughts kept you awake all night as well. All I kept thinking about was how much fear I would be feeling if I was a kid and found out my mom had the same diagnosis. I would be terrified. I did not want that for my kids!

What I realized is that my kids are a lot stronger than I ever was. They are resilient, empathetic, courageous and kind human beings and I firmly believe that they will choose to turn this experience into something that propels them forward instead of holding them back. That's what challenges do, if you are willing to reframe them in a way that works for you. My kids are my heroes. I think of them every single day and am truly inspired by the humans they have become.

Raise your kids to be able to handle life. Don't immediately think that the crisis you are dealing with will pull them under. Encourage them to talk and be open, but be OK with letting them handle it in a way that feels most comfortable for them. Don't panic. The kids are alright.

23
Find your burpee.

Being a fitness instructor who uses social media to build and maintain a business is a double-edged sword. While it can be a great way to connect with people and spread the word about who you are and what you are doing, it also can leave you a little bit vulnerable. It puts you on display. Because of this, I have always found it best to be as honest and real as possible. That way, there are no surprises if someone sees me in "real life." I have always tried to talk the talk and walk the walk, no matter how someone knows me.

That's why, when I was diagnosed with cancer, I felt the need to be as open as possible. I didn't know what the journey would look like and by keeping my diagnosis private, I felt it may lead to people questioning what exactly was going on with me. The last thing I would ever want is for people to think I wasn't taking my job seriously or I was slacking off in some way if I started to feel or look sick.

I would love to tell you that I sat here pondering my announcement for days, but that would be a lie. I came up with the idea in five minutes after I asked my husband for advice about how to do it. The one nugget of advice he gave me was, "Give it a purpose." For some reason, all of a sudden, I thought of a burpee.

What if I made the announcement and then committed to doing one burpee a day until I beat cancer? Surely, that was reasonable and do-able no matter how rotten I felt. It was also a way of me taking a morsel of control over a situation that seemed very much out of my control. It was a way for me to establish a physical norm and check in each day, both for me and my followers. In addition, I thought this would be a good check in for my kids. It would be a way for us to keep our eyes on the horizon if the seas got a little rough. It would be a sign that I was still fighting and on the right track.

So on February 5th, 2024, I did my first burpee and I have continued them each day along my journey. Along the way I started doing an additional burpee for a friend battling breast cancer and sometimes do a third one if someone else needs support. I have burpeed in my house, outside, in the water, in my pjs, in a dress, in crazy wigs, with special guests, at sporting events and even in Target. I've had countless amazing supporters burpee in honor of me on social media, at sporting events, at schools and even show up in my driveway and front lawn to surprise me. Friends have sent me videos of their kids and even their dogs doing a burpee! My favorite burpees have been from my husband Tim, my kids and their friends, and my dear friend, Colleen. Every single one has brought a smile to my face and a tear to my eye.

These burpees have become my own personal rallying cry and reminder that I am stronger than this cancer. They are a reminder to myself, my family and anyone else who cares to pay attention that no matter what, I'm still fighting and I will indeed win.

Find your burpee. Create a daily ritual during your fight that will remind yourself and everyone else who cares about you that you are in it win it. Pick something that resonates with you and then keep going. Every day. Until victory is yours!

24
Take control of the narrative.

To me, there is nothing more scary than feeling out of control. Perhaps that's why I don't like fast speeds or scary roller coasters. I like to be the captain of my own ship. Giving someone else the reins or feeling like I have no say over what's happening to me freaks me out.

I think this is why cancer, or any other type of curve ball that life throws at you can feel so scary. It's terrifying to think that you have no control over what's happening in your body or your life. It's in these moments that I feel it's so important to remember that while we may not be able to change a scary situation we find ourselves in, we *do* have a say in how we react to it. No matter what happens in our lives, we always have the opportunity to create the narrative.

The narrative does not have to be loud. You do not have to share your experiences in a public forum. For some, the narrative may be created in private. The sense of control may come in the form of not sharing and being able to deal with things behind closed doors or with the people closest to you.

For others, the comfort and sense of control may come in the form of publicly sharing their experience through the lens they would like it to be seen through. This can be an excellent opportunity for people to inspire others who may be going through something similar. It can be a way for someone to make sense of and give meaning to something that otherwise makes no sense.

It's important to remember and respect the fact that everyone has their own way of dealing with things. Some find comfort and solace in sharing their experiences, while others prefer privacy to deal with life's challenges. One way is no better than the other. What's important is that you remember not to drown in the situation you find yourself in. It's your responsibility to find the meaning in it instead of succumbing to it.

25
Reframe your situation.

I wrote this post as I was getting ready for my double mastectomy. It seemed to really hit a nerve with a lot of my friends and family, so I wanted to include it here. Being able to reframe your situation by using analogies is one of the greatest coping skills!

I've realized my biggest coping skill comes in the form of being able to create analogies. It's how I make sense of life. When my mind can't comprehend something scary, challenging or sad, I try to relate it to something else I have experienced. Once I do that, I can pull up my big girl pants and formulate a plan to move forward and do whatever needs to be done. The situation starts to feel so familiar, it almost feels like I have a road map.

I will tell you that hearing "You have cancer" was one of my greatest fears (like number 3 on my list... mice is number 4). So when it happened, I had to quickly come up with a way to find some sort of familiarity in a situation that left me feeling like I was lost in the darkness of a dense forest. Then I remembered my triathlons, and it all started to make sense.

Up until this point (getting the cancer diagnosis and all the testing and dealing with all the unknowns), I have spent many days and nights feeling as if I was drowning. That's how I usually feel in the swim for a triathlon. It's scary. All of a sudden you are in the water and no matter how much you have trained for this day, it still makes you feel panicky. You can't see what's in front of you. If you have done a tri and are anything like me, you sometimes start swimming completely off course until you manage to raise your head and spot a buoy to get yourself back on track. It takes a while to make sense of your environment. You have to remind yourself to just take one stroke at a time and to steady your breath. Bottom line, you just do whatever you have to do to make it through.

On Friday, I will be transitioning to the bike part of my journey: surgery and recovery. This is the part of the event I always think is the most annoying. While at first you are so happy to be out of the water, the reality quickly sets in that you will be getting pretty uncomfortable on that bike seat in that hunched over position. I always wish I could just get to the run already, so I can cross the finish line and celebrate my accomplishment (and have a beer haha). The bike is frustrating, just like I can imagine recovering from surgery is going to be. I don't like to sit. But, I promise I will.

Chemo is the run. I'll be honest, the run of the triathlon is always the most grueling for me. That's where my true mental toughness sets in. It's truly mind over matter. No matter how much my knee hurts or stomach cramps and how badly I want to stop, I don't. I always think about how far I have come and how I made it through the scary swim and the boring bike; so it only makes sense to keep going. It's also the part of the race when you start to get closer and closer to that finish line. I can start to imagine how I will feel when I cross it. Those thoughts put fuel in my emptying tank.

I'm posting this to remind you that every challenge you have ever gone through, whether it was by choice or by circumstance, can be used to help you get through *whatever* crazy and scary curveball life throws at you. And if you don't feel like you have ever been challenged, create an obstacle for yourself and practice now!

My cancer journey is my new triathlon. I have been here before. I can do this. I will win.

26

Be someone's frog.

My friend Jenna has a frog that has made a little home in one of her flower pots on her back deck. She checks on it every day, says hello, and makes sure the frog has a little water on hot days. According to Jenna, this frog only leaves the flower pot when she is gone for a few days at a time. Jenna knows this because the frog always returns the day after she gets back from wherever she went. The frog has become Jenna's consistent pal and it brings her joy knowing that the frog seems to understand just how much Jenna enjoys him (or her). It's a sweet bond.

Hearing Jenna explain the situation with her frog made me think of my relationship with Jenna. Jenna and I have known each other for years, but as often happens, life has been so busy that the closest we have ever gotten to doing something together is simply talking about it. When I got my diagnosis, though, Jenna took a huge step forward and quickly became one of my most caring and present friends.

When I was first diagnosed, Jenna sent me a text with four well-thought-out options for us to get together, depending on what I was in the mood for. She let me know she was up for any of them at any time. Just seeing the text made my heart feel lighter. Jenna showed up at my house the day after my surgery with homemade mini-muffins and left them on my doorstep because she didn't want to bother me. When I started chemo, Jenna made it a point to get together with me every other Wednesday (my "off" Wednesdays from chemo), whether it be at my house, or mostly hers. She has consistently paid attention to my symptoms and what I could stomach, and had hot ginger peach tea waiting for me or a refreshing glass of iced tea (in a wine glass) as the weather got warmer. Jenna has even gone so far as to leave me a box of the peach ginger tea and some epsom salts on my doorstep when she knew I was having a tough week.

All of these little gestures have lifted me up on some of my darkest days. Jenna has a lot in common with her little frog. She has stuck by my side and always seems to know exactly when I need her. Knowing she is there has had such a positive impact on my cancer journey. Maybe the frog seems to sense a kindred spirit in Jenna.

The lesson here is twofold. When you are going through a tough time, lean on those "frogs" who show up and make the commitment to be there for you. Sometimes it can open the door to a beautiful new friendship you can't imagine going through life without! And if you are someone in a position similar to Jenna, take that step forward like she did. Be a frog. You have no idea how much strength you will be giving the person who needs it!

27

Appreciate your invisible strings.

There is a very lovely theory out there that is used to explain why some people stay connected, even after long periods of being apart. It's called the "Invisible String Theory." The idea is that fate connects people through an invisible string or cord. I had heard about this theory before I was diagnosed with cancer and became convinced that I had some invisible strings at play connecting me to other people. While I still believe some of those people are connected to me, I realize now that I didn't fully understand the meaning of this theory, until now. I had to come full circle with a very special friend who I thought I had lost forever.

Her name is Lisa. We have been friends since I was four months old and she was one year old. The story goes that when my parents moved in across the street from Lisa's parents, my dad found out Lisa's parents were Norwegian. Being that my mom's parents were from Denmark, the Scandinavian connection seemed like a perfect ice breaker for a neighborhood friendship. My dad wasn't wrong.

Lisa and I grew up with similar Scandinavian traditions. We both loved Christmas Eve more than Christmas Day, as is the way the holiday is celebrated in Denmark and Norway. We both had "Mormors" (mother's mother) and said "Jeg elsker dig" (I love you) to each other often, pretending it was our secret language. Our mothers dressed us in traditional Danish and Norwegian outfits for parties and we loved knowing that our families had something so special in common.

Lisa is part of every single childhood memory I have. She was the guest of honor at all my birthday parties and my first choice for sleepovers. Lisa knew all the key players and family members in my life and was the keeper of all my little girl secrets, dreams and wishes. I remember my mom informing me that not everyone had the same best friend their entire life and I could not fathom that to be true. The idea that not everyone had a "Lisa" in their life made me feel incredibly sad.

Lisa and I spent thirty years walking down the path of life side by side, always aware of each other's presence, but at some point when we weren't paying attention, we became a bit lost. There was never a fight, unkind word or any sort of defining negative moment. We just lost track of each other and couldn't seem to find our way back to one another. It bothered me, but I didn't know what exactly to do about it so I just buried the feelings of loss deep down inside and covered them up with the busyness of life. For the next fifteen years, I made wonderful new friends and kept telling myself it was ok to move on.

On February 2nd, I was diagnosed with breast cancer and made the decision to let my family and close friends know right away. The first person I thought of, besides my immediate family, was Lisa. It had been 15 years since we had a meaningful conversation or spent any significant time together. She had never even met my younger son. I kept thinking of how I would feel if she was the one diagnosed and didn't tell me. I would be crushed. I picked up my phone and texted her the news.

From that moment, Lisa has entered back into my life like no time has passed. She has called and/or texted me every single day to make sure I'm okay physically, mentally and emotionally. She texts my husband to check in on him and asks how my kids are doing. She's taken the trip up to visit me, once after my surgery and another time to take me to chemo. During the summer of my chemo treatments when I was visiting my parents in NJ, she picked me up and took me to the beach during a very sick time and came over to float with me in the pool when I was too exhausted to do anything else. She has been one of the main pillars of support in my life and I don't know what I would do without her.

Rekindling this special friendship has made me realize and admit how much I had been missing it all these years, but it has also proven the "Invisible String" theory in such a beautiful way. We have been and always will be connected. Our fates are intertwined. I know I can count on that now and it's one of the greatest silver linings of this whole journey I've been on.

Believe in those invisible strings that are attaching you to the special people in your life. Take them seriously. Those are the people that can carry you through the most difficult times.

28

Be a soul sister.

When I studied abroad in Denmark, I kept a journal; and if you read the pages, there are two things that are clearly evident. The first one is that I was one hell of a hot mess. The second one is that I absolutely idolized my host mother, Grethe Hansen.

Pretty much every single page includes sentences like, "Grethe said…" or "Grethe thinks…" or "Grethe took me to…". Being placed with her completely at random, only enhances my belief in guardian angels. Looking back, I was really at a pretty serious crossroads in my life, and this experience had the potential to make or break me. Thanks to Grethe, my time in Denmark helped shape who I am today and has been a huge source of comfort to me on my cancer journey.

Grethe and I have a ton of special memories together, but there is one memory that stands out in my mind and sums up the way I feel about her. It's also something I have reflected on during my sleepless and anxiety ridden nights since my diagnosis. I had been traveling with friends on Spring break and came home to Værløse, Denmark. Grethe and her husband were traveling as well and wouldn't be home until later that day. It was a typical chilly Danish spring day, but the sun was bright and had warmed the patio in their garden. I was exhausted so I grabbed a pillow and just laid down on the warm cement and fell asleep. I remember being somewhere between sleep and awake when I started to feel cold. And then I felt a blanket being put over me. I didn't open my eyes, but I knew it was Grethe. I remember sensing her quietly sitting down at the table next to where I was laying, flipping the pages of a magazine and I had this sense of being so well taken care of. I just wanted to soak it in and have time stand still for a little while.

Twenty-five years later, I still have that feeling when I'm sitting with Grethe, enjoying perfectly made coffee and exquisite breakfasts in her garden or biking the streets of Copenhagen or the hills of Bornholm. I also carry the feeling with me in my heart, so it exists even with an ocean and years of not seeing each other in between us.

Never underestimate the lifelong effect you can have on a person just by being there for them when they need you most. Be a soul sister. Be like Grethe.

29

It's okay to be scared.

I'll never forget waking up the morning after I had been diagnosed with breast cancer. There is a counted cross-stitch picture on my wall across from my bed, and I remember looking at it and realizing it would never look the same again. Obviously, the picture had not miraculously changed overnight, but the eyes looking at it had. The colors didn't seem quite as vibrant and the funny saying, which usually made me smile, instead made me feel really sad. I rolled over to my husband, put my head on his chest and wept.

My brain didn't know how to make sense of the situation I was in. I had the diagnosis, but there was still so much that was unknown. I remember moving through my days like I was walking through pea soup, both mentally and physically. One moment I felt certain I would conquer whatever was in front of me and then the next moment I felt like curling into a ball and hiding under the covers. It was a constant see-saw of emotions.

The only thing I was certain of is that I didn't want to be in the situation I was in. I spent most of my days and nights simply wishing I wasn't dealing with it. I went over everything I could have done to cause this situation. Did I eat too much sugar? Did I stand too close to the microwave? Did I use too many products with chemicals? Maybe it was all my infertility treatments! Or could it have been the diet soda I used to drink when I was younger? It sounds a little bit crazy, but I thought maybe if I could figure out the reason for the tumor, I may be able to come up with a solution to fix everything. I didn't want to admit this was really happening.

I put on my brave face during the day, but on the inside I was a complete disaster. I was sad, exhausted, angry, confused and overwhelmed. There was one emotion, however, that I was refusing to acknowledge. Whenever it came bubbling up, I would push it down because it felt so incredibly awful and it seemed to exacerbate all the other emotions I was dealing with. The feeling I couldn't seem to acknowledge or admit is that I was completely and utterly *terrified*.

What if I died? How could I leave my kids or my husband? Those were the two questions I just couldn't bring myself to consider.

I would like to tell you that one day I had some amazing breakthrough, dealt with my fear, and it all made sense, but I can't. Because I'm still terrified. But, what this journey has taught me is that it's okay to be scared. You can be terrified and live a happy life at the same time. I can now ask myself those really hard questions and not reach for the Ativan. It just takes a little while to come to terms with unexpected situations and the feelings that go along with them.

If you are facing something terrifying, remember that you can be sad, happy, brave, scared, confused, clear, in control and out of control all at the same time. The truth is, life is scary for everyone. Nothing is guaranteed. Be patient with yourself, make the most of everyday and fight the good fight the best you can.

30

A little bit about chemo...

Imagine being on a roller coaster ride that malfunctioned so it makes it impossible to get off no matter how loud you are screaming to stop the ride.

One day you feel strong, positive and like nothing can stop you from beating "the bear."

And the next day everything seems like too much, your body hurts in weird ways and all you want to do is escape your current reality.

I have made it my mission to *move* through chemo. That commitment to myself has helped me get through this in so many ways, but it's still very hard.and has given me a whole new perspective and massive respect for anyone and everyone who has gone through this before me.

Everyone's roller coaster ride through chemo and cancer is going to look a little different. Some may have more twists and turns, others may have more extreme ups and downs, and a few may even seem a little less extreme. Regardless of what it looks like, it's all hard.

I have found a nugget of strength in everyone's story, even if they are handling it in a completely different way than me.

No matter what kind of cancer roller coaster you are on or will be on, bring that lap bar down, hold on tight, take a deep breath and remember: **YOU GOT THIS**.

31

Pick your tribe.

One of the great things about being so open and public about my breast cancer diagnosis was that I was immediately connected to some of the most amazing cancer survivors. It seemed that most of my friends knew someone who had been on a similar breast cancer journey and were very willing to make the introduction. I was also invited and welcomed with open arms to many Facebook groups of cancer survivors. I think that welcoming support has been one of the nicest things people have done to help me, and I will always be grateful.

The truth is, there are many different kinds of breast cancer. If you Google it, you will see all the different types and within those types there are of course varying stages and grades. I actually *do not* recommend you Google it because it can be very scary and overwhelming. In the beginning, it was so helpful to talk to anyone who was going through or who had survived breast cancer. My goal was to arm myself with as much information as possible. I found that talking to people was the best way for me to learn how to navigate this new world I had been thrust into and a great tool for me to make sense of my thoughts and feelings about it. That was until I started to get extremely overwhelmed.

I found myself constantly comparing my diagnosis to other people's and trying to decide if it was "better" or "worse." I became slightly envious of those who didn't have to go through chemo and a bit unnerved by others who seemed to have a rougher road. The more I learned about my specific cancer, the more I solely relied on those who could completely relate to the exact journey I was on and had gone through my exact diagnosis. I found comfort in two of the most amazing, resilient, no nonsense, tell it like it is, triple negative breast cancer survivors in the whole entire world: Maggie & Nikki.

Maggie was a UCONN lacrosse teammate of my sister in law, Abbey. I had remembered Abbey telling me about Maggie's brave battle against breast cancer a few years earlier, but of course it didn't mean as much to me then as it meant to me after I was diagnosed. Abbey reached out to me the day after I got the dreaded call from my doctor and told me that Maggie was expecting my call. I'll be honest. I don't remember calling her. I was in such a dark place at that moment, it literally felt like someone had shut all the lights off and I was walking around in pitch black. I do remember, though, the second Maggie picked up the phone and started talking. She had me laughing five minutes in with her blunt honesty and stories about how she created an 80's style family Christmas card based on an amazing wig she found. She'd had her husband and kids dress in tracksuits and pose in a way that completely matched the awkward era. She told me the most important thing I needed to do at that moment was believe I was going to be okay. When I hung up with her, the darkness had lifted. The light was turned back on and I felt an incredible surge of hope that I have carried with me throughout this journey. Maggie is a strong survivor who taught me to be one, too.

I had met Nikki a few years earlier through a yoga studio where I worked. I had heard tales of her courageous battle against triple negative breast cancer as a very young woman who just had her first child. I remember a few years later, after she kicked cancer's ass, she took boxing lessons and entered the ring to raise money for breast cancer research. When I spoke with her, I was in awe of the balance of her strength and kindness. It had been a couple of years since we had seen each other, but when she heard I was diagnosed with cancer, she reached out to me to let me know I could talk to her anytime. I'll never forget the day I got a message from a woman I didn't even know telling me that triple negative cancer was one of the worst diagnoses you could get. It sent me down a mental rabbit hole I was desperately trying to stay out of. I reached out to Nikki and within 10 minutes she texted me back research disproving all of the woman's comments to me.

She let me know that if that ever happened again, she would always be there to pull me out of the hole. Nikki is a fearless warrior who taught me to be one, too.

If you are going through something hard, take the time to find the people who have been where you are. Find those who have walked in shoes as similar to yours as possible. No two people's journeys are exactly the same, but there is so much comfort in finding those who truly understand your situation and are willing to share, understand, explain, commiserate, remind, make you laugh and love you in a way nobody else can. Pick your tribe and hold on tight.

32

A final word about your journey.

There is a scene in the movie "The Hurt Locker" where Jeremy Renner, who has just returned home from combat in Iraq, is standing in a grocery store cereal aisle. He finds himself unable to physically move down the aisle because he's so overwhelmed by the choices and contrast between what he has just been through and where he is now. He just stands there. Staring. This scene has been playing over and over in my mind lately because I can relate to his mental anguish. To be honest, I have felt like I have been standing in that exact cereal aisle since finishing chemo.

I thought my last day of chemo was going to be a huge celebration. I imagined the relief and excitement I would feel having some of the most challenging days of my life behind me. I considered it a closure on a chapter of my life I didn't really want to read anymore. So when I got home from chemo, sat on the couch and started crying, I was kind of shocked. The happiness I was so looking forward to feeling was nowhere to be found. In its place,

I felt sheer terror, along with a deluge of questions running through my head. What if the cancer comes back? What if I have to do chemo all over again? What if someone I love gets sick? How can I just be on my own now? Shouldn't I be taking a pill or something to prevent a recurrence? Why do my teeth hurt? Did the cancer spread to my gums?

And then came the wave of guilt. I started thinking of every person I met in the chemo room at Dana Farber who happened to be on a much more brutal journey than mine. I thought of the woman who had been doing chemo for two years and had no end in sight. I thought of the man whose cancer has spread to his bones and was living on borrowed time. I thought of the single mom who had little kids and was trying to wrap her brain around how she was going to take care of her babies and fight cancer at the same time. I could see myself in every story and felt terribly uncomfortable knowing I had a ton of hope in my journey, but still couldn't seem to enjoy it. I had come up too close for comfort to my own mortality and that was really hard to make sense of.

What I started to realize over the next couple of days was that the journey I had been on since February, when I got my diagnosis, was not over and it never will be. It's just entering a different phase. I will never be the same Carly I was before all this happened. It's going to take some time for me to unpack the last six months. I need to figure out a new place for all the memories and emotions because the space I have known up until this point hasn't had to accommodate them. In order to cope, I have had to put on blinders and armor and push forward in the only way I know how. Somehow I have to remember how to feel and not have it send me into a complete panic. I need to be patient with myself.

Struggles, challenges, and tragedies change us. Even if there is a happy ending, it can take some time to actually feel anything close to relief or joy. Our eyes have been opened to new thoughts, feelings, and fears. We've witnessed things we never imagined, and that can be completely overwhelming to the body, mind, and soul. It's okay to be confused. It's okay to be sad. It's okay to wish things were different. Feel the feels. Allow yourself some grace. Take the time you need and don't be afraid to talk about it with the ones you love. You will get through this.

And always… *Pray for the Bear.*

Acknowledgments

Thank you so much for choosing to read this book! It has been very therapeutic and a labor of love for me to write during my journey. I would like to thank my editor, Carolyn Wynn, for being so willing to help me during this process, always cheering for me and giving me so much support! I could not have done it without her. I would also like to thank my publishing consultant, D. Patrick Miller, for understanding how much this project means to me and being so willing to work with me to make it happen.

And of course, I could not have done this without the daily support from Tim (my husband), Chris (my brother) and my parents! I'm extremely grateful for their love.